SPECTRUM
READERS

W9-ADU-317

AMAZING!

Carson-Dellosa
Publishing

SPECTRUM®

An imprint of Carson-Dellosa Publishing, LLC
P.O. Box 35665
Greensboro, NC 27425-5665

carsondellosa.com

Printed in the USA. All rights reserved.
ISBN 978-1-62399-159-3

01-179137784

Guided Reading Level: J

WILD!
Animal
Journeys

By Katharine Kenah

Some animals live in one place.
Some animals move from place to place.
They move to find food.
They move to find warm weather.
They move to find safety.
Animals that move migrate.
Some animals take amazing journeys!

Arctic Tern

Arctic terns are on the move!
They fly from the top of the world
to the bottom—and back—every year.
The distance is equal to circling
the earth one time.

Canada Goose

Canada geese are on the move!
A flock of geese fly in a V shape.
The V shape helps all the birds
stay together.
Canada geese fly north in the spring.
They fly south to warm weather
in the fall.

Starling

Starlings are on the move!
Starlings migrate during the day
and night.
By day, starlings follow rivers
and shorelines.
By night, starlings follow the moon
and stars.
Once a young starling makes its first
migration, it seems to remember
the trip the next time.

Gray Whale

Gray whales are on the move!
In summer, gray whales swim
in cold water near the North Pole.
They eat and store up fat,
called *blubber*.
In winter, they swim south
to the warm water near Mexico.

Sea Turtle

Sea turtles are on the move!
When sea turtles are ready to lay eggs,
they swim over 1,000 miles.
They swim to the beaches
where they were born.
They lay eggs in holes in the sand.
Then, they return to the sea.

Salmon

Salmon are on the move!
Salmon are born in streams.
Then, they swim out to the ocean
to live.
When it is time to lay eggs,
some adult salmon swim 2,000 miles
back to the stream where
they were born.

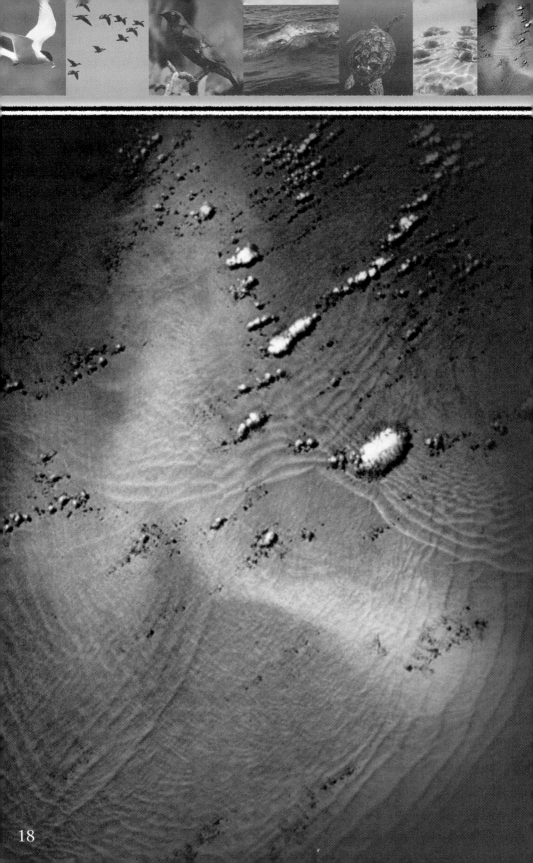

Zooplankton

Zooplankton are on the move!
Zooplankton are very tiny animals.
They live near the top of the sea.
Zooplankton migrate every day.
They swim down
when the sun comes out.
They swim up
when the sky grows dark.

Earthworm

Earthworms are on the move!
During cold weather, earthworms
crawl down deep into the ground.
The dirt is warm and wet there.
In warm weather, they crawl up again.
The dirt is warmer near the surface.

Desert Locust

Desert locusts are on the move!
They move in groups called *swarms*.
One swarm may have billions
of locusts.
This is one locust for almost every
person on earth.
Migrating swarms can grow so large
that they block out the sunlight!

Monarch Butterfly

Monarch butterflies are on the move!
In September, monarch butterflies fly
from Canada to Mexico.
They fly towards warm weather.
In March, monarch butterflies
fly north again.
They fly close to 2,000 miles!

Caribou

Caribou are on the move!
Caribou migrate around
the Arctic Circle.
This is the cold spot
at the top of the world.
Caribou walk hundreds of miles.
They look for food to eat.
They look for places to give birth.

African Elephant

African elephants are on the move!
They migrate over large, grassy spaces.
They look for food and water.
Elephants are called
"gardeners of Africa."
They drop seeds as they eat plants
and move.

Serengeti Migration

Millions of animals are on the move!
The Serengeti is a national park
in Tanzania, Africa.
It is the size of the state of Connecticut!
Zebras, gazelles, and wildebeest
migrate around the park each year.
They move to find food and water.

Bedouin

People are on the move, too!
Bedouins (BEH-du-wins) live in hot,
dry lands.
They live in tents.
They tend herds of animals.
They move to find water and grass
for their animals.

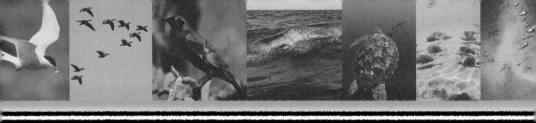

WILD! Animal Journeys Comprehension Questions

1. Why do some animals move from place to place?

2. What does *migrate* mean?

3. Why do Canada geese fly in a V shape?

4. Where do Canada geese fly in the fall?

5. Where do gray whales swim in the summer? What are they doing in the summer?

6. Where do sea turtles lay eggs? What do they do after they lay eggs?

7. Where are salmon born? Where do salmon live?

8. How often do zooplankton migrate?

9. Why are African elephants called "gardeners of Africa"?

10. What is the Serengeti?

CREEPY!
Crawlers

Table of Contents

You might think a spider is an insect.
You might think a tick is an insect, too.
But they are not!
These creatures belong to
another animal family.
They are arachnids (uh RACK nidz).

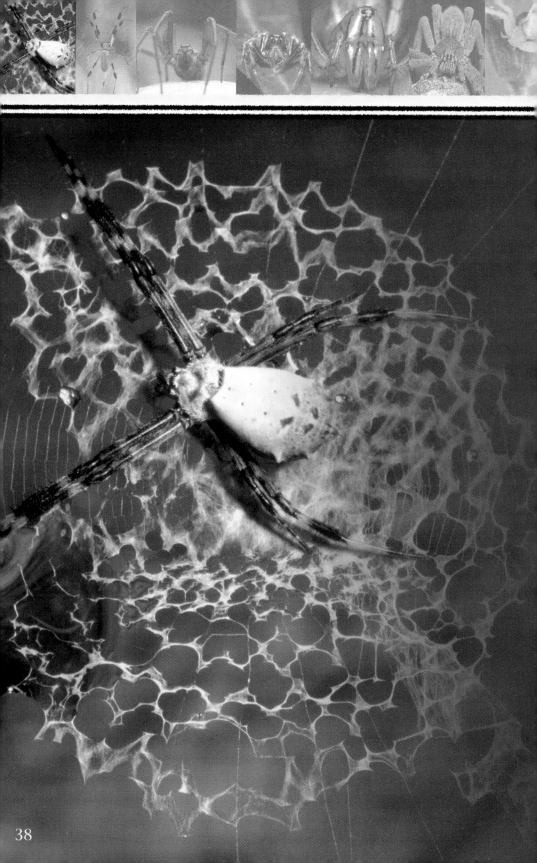

Orb Weaver Spider

What does this arachnid do?
It makes strings of silk.
Then, it spins the strings of silk
into a round web.
You might see a spider web like this
in your backyard.

Golden Silk Spider

What does this arachnid do?
It traps insects in its web.
The insects stick to the gooey silk.
They become food for the spider.

Wolf Spider

What does this arachnid do?
It hunts for food.
It bites its prey with sharp teeth.
These teeth are called *fangs*.

Jumping Spider

What does this arachnid do?
It sneaks up on insects.
Then, it jumps on them and eats them.
The jumping spider also jumps
away from danger.

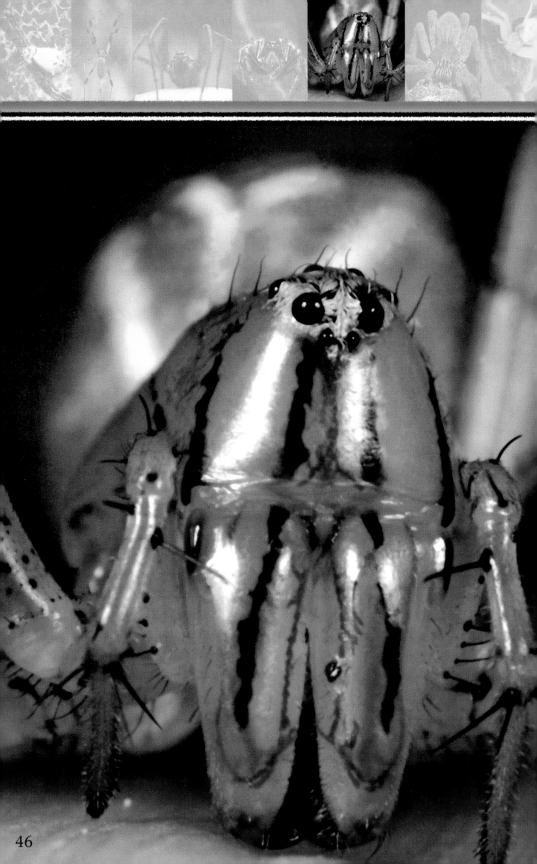

Lynx Spider

What does this arachnid do?
It runs quickly over plants and flowers.
The lynx spider chases insects.
Sometimes, it leaps out and
surprises them.

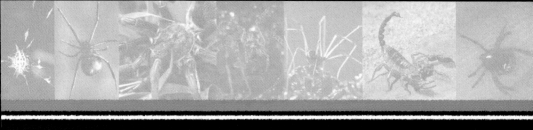

Huntsman Spider

What does this arachnid do?
It hides in trees.
Its brown color looks like tree bark.
This makes it hard for other animals
to see the huntsman spider.

Crab Spider

What does this arachnid do?
Sometimes, it changes color!
A crab spider hides in flowers.
It can change its color to blend in
with a flower's bright blooms.

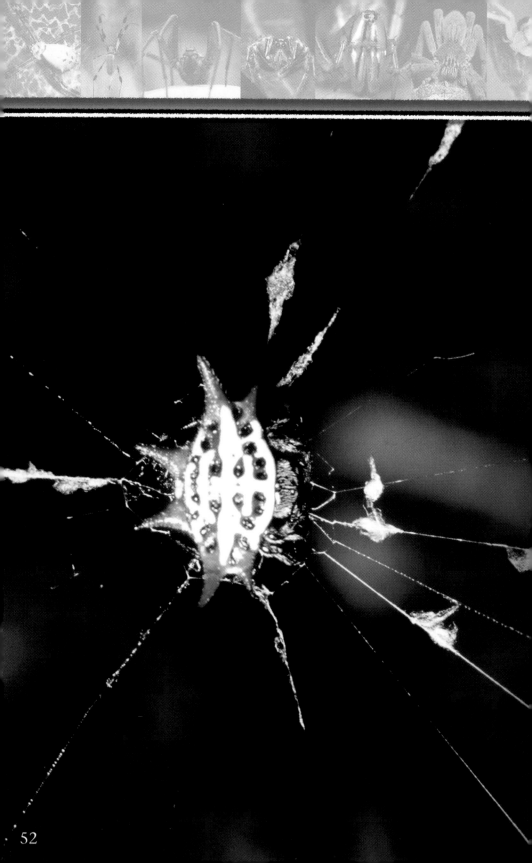

Jewel Spider

What does this arachnid do?
It keeps birds away.
Birds do not want to eat
the jewel spider.
It has pointy spines on its body!

Black Widow Spider

What does this arachnid do?
Sometimes, it bites.
Most spiders don't bite people.
But once in a while, the black
widow does.
Its bite can make a person very sick!

Tarantula

What does this arachnid do?
It grows and grows.
Tarantulas are the largest kinds
of spiders in the world.
Some are as big as your hand!

Grass Spider

What does this arachnid do?
It hides in its web.
It waits for an insect to crawl onto it.
Then, it runs quickly to catch it.

Daddy Longlegs

What does this arachnid do?
It crawls quickly.
A daddy longlegs has eight
long, thin legs.
It looks a lot like a spider,
but it is a different kind of arachnid.

Scorpion

What does this arachnid do?
It stings.
The scorpion has a sharp stinger
on the end of its tail.
It also has pointy claws
called *pincers* (PIN surz).

Tick

What does this arachnid do?
It crawls onto another animal.
It bites the animal and drinks
its blood.
That is how the tick gets its food!

CREEPY! Crawlers
Comprehension Questions

1. What animal family does a spider belong to?

2. What does an orb weaver spider make?

3. What does a wolf spider use to bite its prey?

4. Do you think a jumping spider uses a web to catch food?

5. What color is the huntsman spider? Why is that color helpful?

6. Why do you think the jewel spider got its name?

7. Which spiders are the largest spiders in the world? How big are these spiders?

8. Is a daddy longlegs a spider?

9. What are a scorpion's pointy claws called?

10. How does a tick get its food?

DANGER!
Deadly Animals

Table of Contents

Some small things make you say,
"Come quick! Look at this."
A puppy.
A butterfly.
A starfish.

But some small things make you say,
"Stay away! Do not come near."
Turn the page to meet
some little monsters.

Blue Poison Dart Frog

Look high in the tree.
What do you see?

The frog that you see is
the color of the sky.
Do not touch it.
Its skin is covered with poison.

Blue-Ringed Octopus

Look into the tide pool.
What do you see?

The octopus that you see is
no longer than your finger.
Do not touch it.
If its rings are blue, it may bite you.

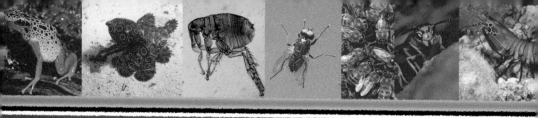

Flea

Look on your pet.
What do you see?

The flea that you see is
smaller than a grain of rice.
Do not touch it.
It may bite you.

Fly

Look at your lunch.
What do you see?

The fly that you see is
tasting your lunch.
It is using its feet to taste.
Do not touch it.
Flies carry lots of germs.

Killer Bee

Look on the flower.
What do you see?

The bee that you see is
a kind of honeybee.
It guards its hive and honey well.
Do not touch one.
Bees like this one sting.

Hornet

Look under that roof.
What do you see?

The hornet that you see builds a nest.
The nest is shaped like a football.
Hornets make their nests out of paper.
Do not touch one.
A hornet stings again and again.

Mantis Shrimp

Look into the water.
What do you see?

The mantis shrimp
that you see is fast.
It is a mighty fighter.
Do not touch one.
Its sharp claws can cut you.

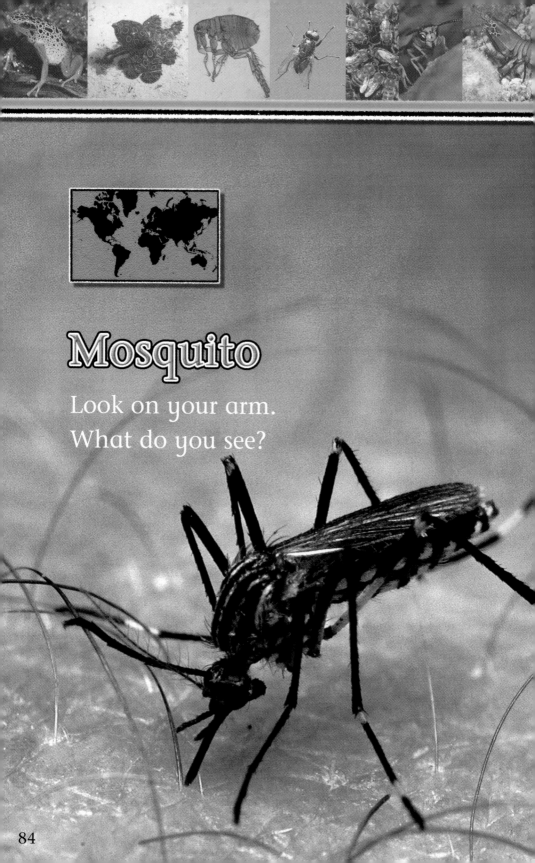

Mosquito

Look on your arm.
What do you see?

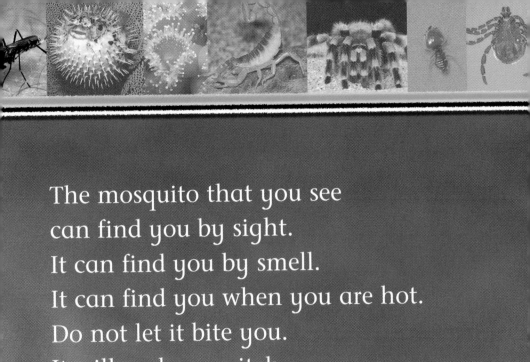

The mosquito that you see
can find you by sight.
It can find you by smell.
It can find you when you are hot.
Do not let it bite you.
It will make you itch.

Puffer Fish

Look into the ocean.
What do you see?

The puffer fish that you see puffs up.
It puffs up when it senses danger.
Do not eat one!
A puffer fish is full of poison.

Sea Anemone

Look at that coral reef.
What do you see?

The sea anemone that you see
looks like a flower.
It moves in the water to catch food.
Do not touch one.
It will sting you.

89

Scorpion

Look on that sunny rock.
What do you see?

The scorpion that you see
likes warm, dark places.
It hunts at night.
Do not touch one.
The scorpion has poison in its tail.

Tarantula

Look in that hole.
What do you see?

The spider that you see
is a tarantula.
It is as big as a hand.
Do not poke one.
A tarantula will bite you.

Termite

Look in the wood.
What do you see?

The termite that you see
makes its tall home out of mud.
Termites that live in a group
are called a *colony*.
Do not keep them in your house!
A colony of termites can
chew up a whole house.

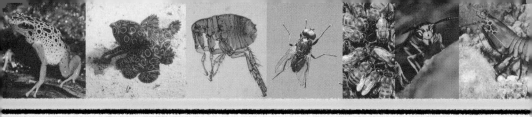

Tick

Look on that deer.
What do you see?

The tick that you see is tiny.
It looks like a raisin with legs.
Do not touch one.
A tick sucks your blood.
It can make you sick.

DANGER! Deadly Animals
Comprehension Questions

1. Why do you think the blue poison dart frog was given its name?

2. How long is the blue-ringed octopus?

3. Do you think a flea would be easy to see?

4. Why should you not touch a flea?

5. What does a fly use to taste?

6. What is a hornet nest shaped like?

7. When does the puffer fish puff up?

8. Why should you not eat a puffer fish?

9. What does a sea anemone look like?

10. Why should you not keep termites in your house?

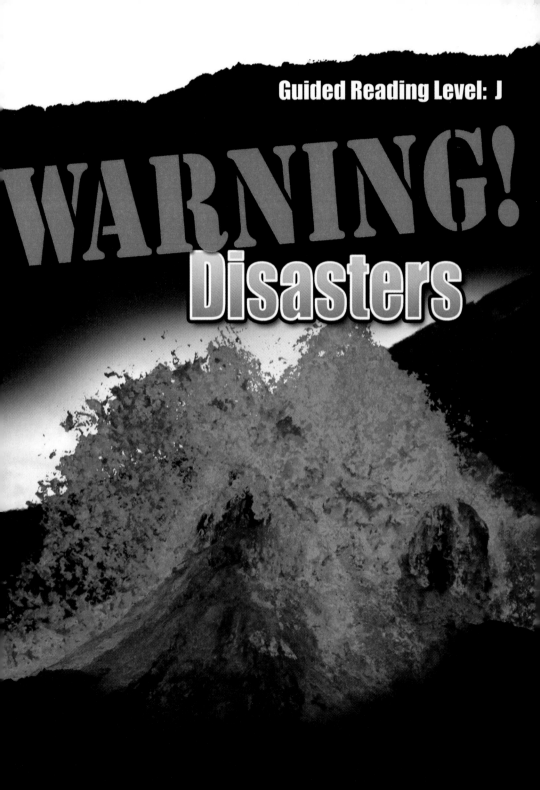

WARNING!
Disasters

By Katharine Kenah

Table of Contents

On earth, some places are hot.
Some places are cold.
Some places are wet.
Some places are dry.

But one thing is the same.
These places all change.
Sometimes, these changes
can be destructive!

Volcano

The sky is turning black.
What is happening?

A volcano is blowing its top!
Dirt fills the air.
Rivers of red-hot melted rock
flow downhill.
This rock is called *lava*.
It comes from inside the earth.

Continental Drift

You cannot feel it,
but the earth is moving.
What is happening?

Mountains are being made!
The earth is like an egg.
It has a shell.
Scientists think the earth's shell
is made of pieces, called *plates*.
These pieces move very slowly.
When two plates hit, mountains
can form.

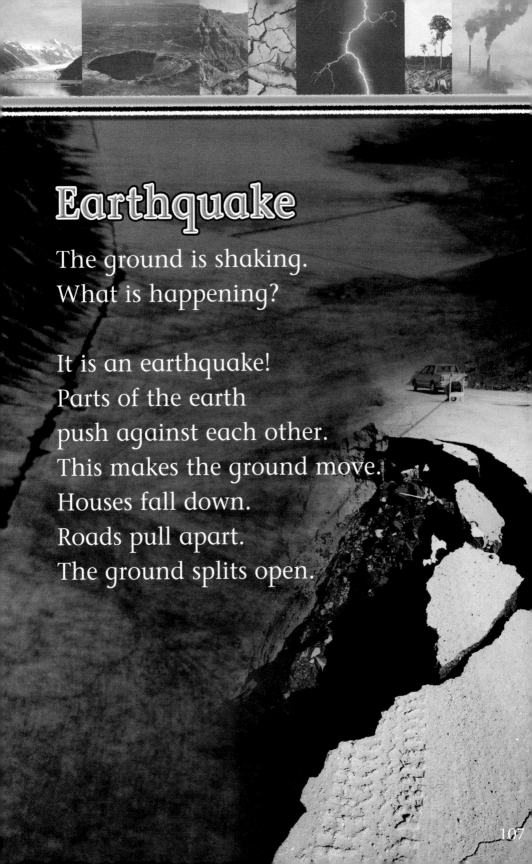

Earthquake

The ground is shaking.
What is happening?

It is an earthquake!
Parts of the earth
push against each other.
This makes the ground move.
Houses fall down.
Roads pull apart.
The ground splits open.

Tsunami

A huge wall of water is coming.
What is happening?

A tsunami is hitting!
There is an earthquake
under the ocean floor.
It shakes the land and the water.
It makes a huge wave race
toward the shore.

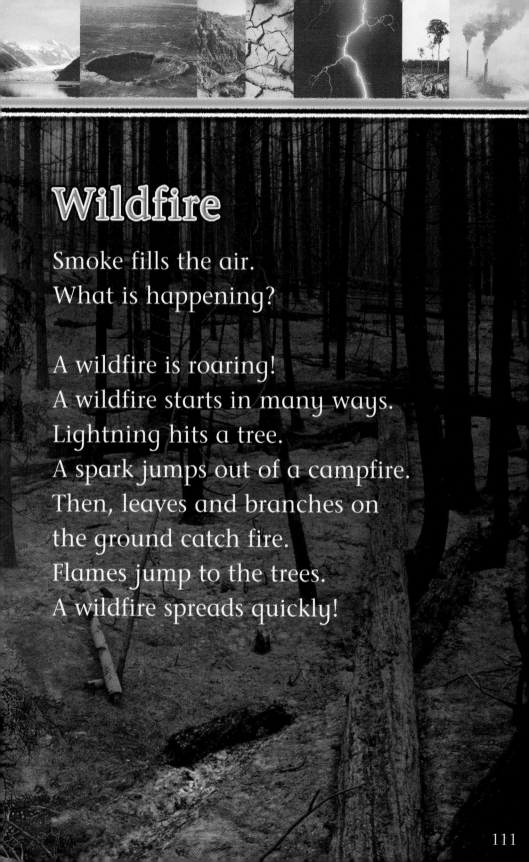

Wildfire

Smoke fills the air.
What is happening?

A wildfire is roaring!
A wildfire starts in many ways.
Lightning hits a tree.
A spark jumps out of a campfire.
Then, leaves and branches on
the ground catch fire.
Flames jump to the trees.
A wildfire spreads quickly!

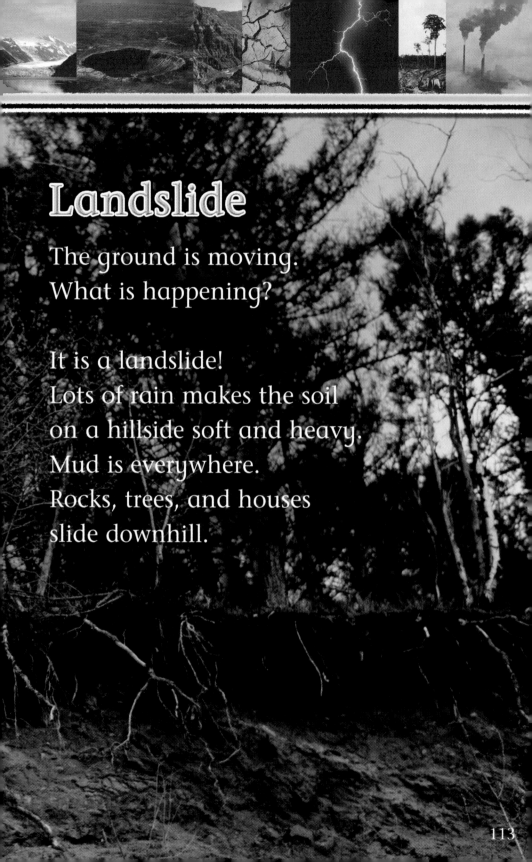

Landslide

The ground is moving.
What is happening?

It is a landslide!
Lots of rain makes the soil
on a hillside soft and heavy.
Mud is everywhere.
Rocks, trees, and houses
slide downhill.

Avalanche

A snow cloud is coming.
What is happening?

An avalanche is dropping!
Snow is deep on a mountain.
Strong winds blow it.
Skiers cross over it.
Suddenly, the snow breaks loose.
It races down the mountain.
It covers everything in its
path with snow.

Glacier

Ice is everywhere.
What is happening?

A glacier is moving!
Snow turns to ice.
The ice moves like a river.
It flows slowly downhill.
A glacier cuts away hills and rock.
It creates its own path.

Meteor Impact

There is a big dent in the earth,
shaped like a bowl.
What is it?

A meteorite hit the earth!
Every day, rocks fall from space.
Most of them burn up
above the earth.
But sometimes,
one hits the ground.

Erosion

Water and wind wear away land.
What is happening?

Erosion!
Erosion takes a long time.
It does not happen quickly.
A small river flows downhill.
It makes a path across the ground.
Over millions of years,
the little river cuts away
a giant canyon!

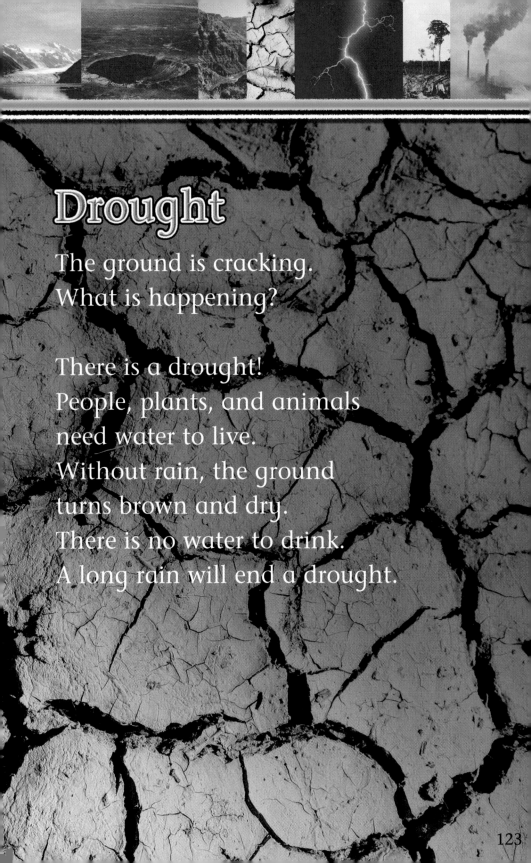

Drought

The ground is cracking.
What is happening?

There is a drought!
People, plants, and animals
need water to live.
Without rain, the ground
turns brown and dry.
There is no water to drink.
A long rain will end a drought.

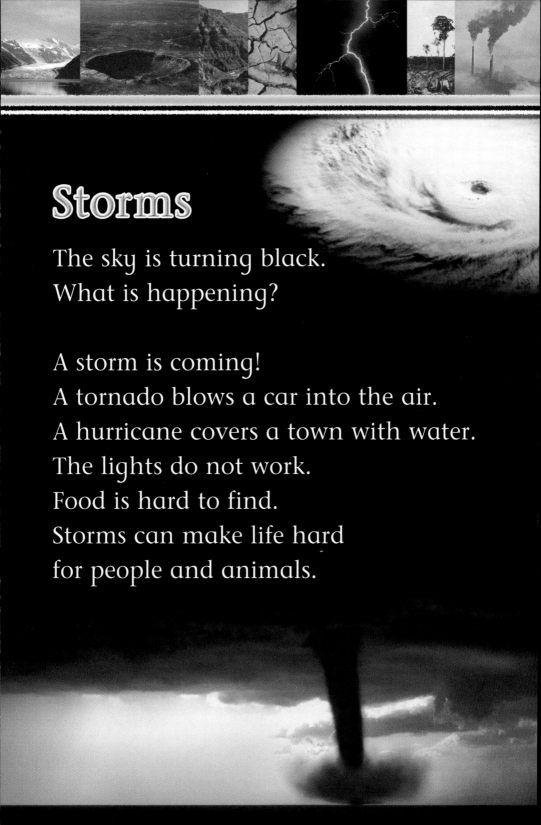

Storms

The sky is turning black.
What is happening?

A storm is coming!
A tornado blows a car into the air.
A hurricane covers a town with water.
The lights do not work.
Food is hard to find.
Storms can make life hard
for people and animals.

Habitat Destruction

The forest is gone.
What is happening?

Animals are losing their homes!
Cities are growing bigger.
More and more people live on earth.
Trees are cut down.
Fields are filling with houses.
Wild animals have no place to go.

Pollution

A seabird is caught in an oil spill.
Factory smoke makes the air
unsafe to breathe.
Trash fills a field.
What is happening?

People are polluting the earth!
They are destroying places
that should be saved.
We must take good care of the earth
and all its living things.

WARNING! Disasters
Comprehension Questions

1. What is lava? Where does it come from?

2. How is the earth like an egg?

3. How are mountains formed?

4. What causes an earthquake? What is the effect of an earthquake?

5. What happens when there is an earthquake under the ocean floor?

6. Why do you think a wildfire can spread quickly?

7. When might a landslide happen?

8. Where does a meteorite come from?

9. Do you think you could see erosion as it happens?

10. Why can storms make life hard for people and animals?

EXTREME!
Earth

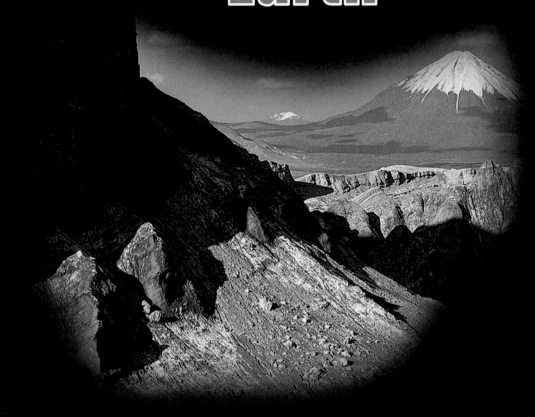

Table of Contents

Where on earth are the
hottest, coldest,
highest, deepest,
largest, and smallest places?

Turn the page to find out.

The Strongest Wind

Where on earth is the strongest wind?
The strongest wind ever recorded hit
a weather station in New Hampshire.
It recorded a wind of 231 miles per hour!
This is faster than most race cars.

135

The Highest Waterfall

Where on earth is the highest waterfall?
The highest waterfall is in South America.
It is called *Angel Falls*.
It is over 3,000 feet tall,
the length of ten football fields!

The Largest Desert

Where on earth is the largest desert?
The largest desert is in North Africa.
It is called the *Sahara Desert*.
For thousands of miles, there is little
to see but sand.

The Largest Island

Where on earth is the largest island?
The largest island is in the
Atlantic Ocean.
It is called *Greenland*.
Greenland is covered with ice.
It is three times bigger than Texas!

The Deepest Lake

Where on earth is the deepest lake?
The deepest lake is in Russia.
It is called *Lake Baikal*.
It is deeper than the Grand Canyon!

The Largest Coral Reef

Where on earth is the largest coral reef?
The largest coral reef is in Australia.
It is called the *Great Barrier Reef*.
It is 1,240 miles long,
the distance from Chicago to Miami.

145

The Longest River

Where on earth is the longest river?
The longest river is in Africa.
It is called the *Nile River.*
It flows for more than 4,000 miles,
the length of South America!

The Most Active Volcano

Where on earth is the most
active volcano?
The most active volcano is in Hawaii.
It is called *Kilauea*.
It has been erupting since 1983!

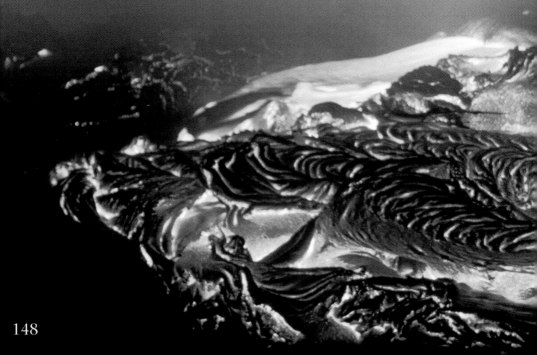

The Longest Cave

Where on earth is the longest cave?
The longest cave is in Kentucky.
It is called *Mammoth Cave*.
There are lakes, rivers, and waterfalls
inside it.

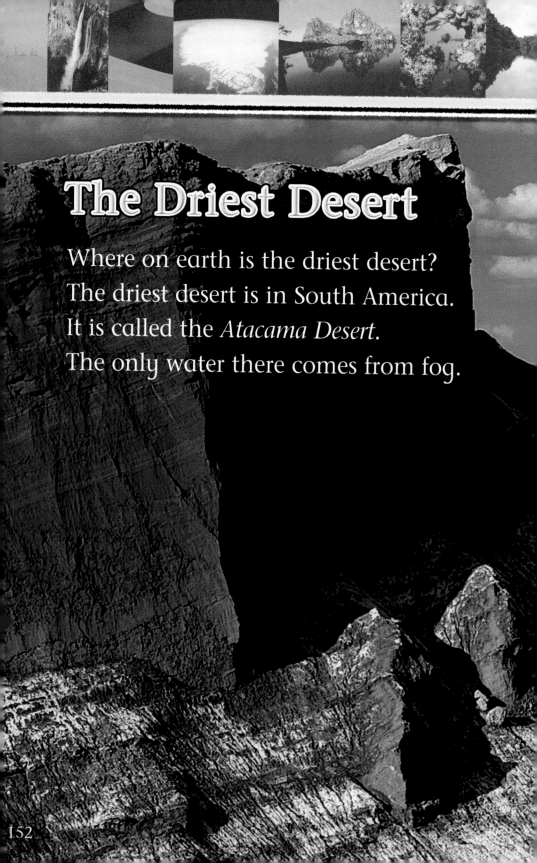

The Driest Desert

Where on earth is the driest desert?
The driest desert is in South America.
It is called the *Atacama Desert*.
The only water there comes from fog.

153

The Deepest Canyon

Where on earth is the deepest canyon?
The deepest canyon is in
South America.
It is called *Colca Canyon*.
It is two miles deep!

The Hottest and Coldest Places

Where on earth are the hottest
and coldest places?
The hottest place is in North America.
It is called *Death Valley*.
The coldest place is at the bottom
of the world.
It is the continent Antarctica.

The Smallest and Largest Continents

Where on earth are the smallest
and largest continents?
The largest continent is Asia.
One-third of the world's land is in Asia.
The smallest continent is Australia.
It is the only country that is also
a continent.

The Largest and Smallest Oceans

Where on earth are the largest and
smallest oceans?

The largest ocean is the Pacific Ocean.
It covers more than one-third of
the world.

The smallest ocean is the Arctic Ocean.
It is almost all ice.

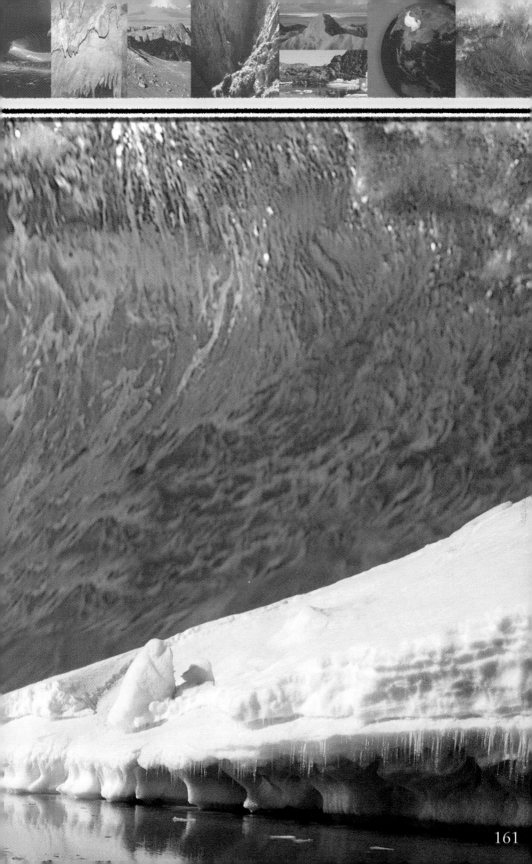

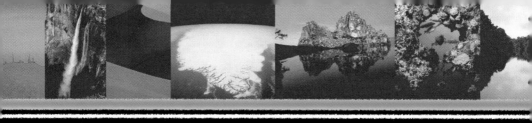

EXTREME! Earth
Comprehension Questions

1. Where was the strongest wind ever recorded?

2. How tall is Angel Falls?

3. Where is Greenland? Do you think you would like to visit Greenland? Why or why not?

4. What is the deepest lake called?

5. Where is the Great Barrier Reef? It is as long as the distance between what two cities?

6. The Nile River is as long as what continent?

7. How long has the most active volcano been erupting?

8. What can you find inside Mammoth Cave?

9. Would you rather visit the hottest or coldest place on Earth? Why?

LOOK CLOSELY!
Hidden
Animals

Table of Contents

Some animals hide
to stay safe from enemies.
They change color.
They change shape.
They have spots.
They have stripes.

Turn the page to see how some
animals hide in the wild.

Polar Bear

Look closely. What do you see?
You see a polar bear and its cub.
They live in a land of ice and snow.
White fur keeps them warm.
It also makes them hard to see.

Stick Insect

Look closely. What do you see?
You see a stick insect.
A small head and a long,
thin body make it hard to see.
It looks like a tree branch.

Gecko

Look closely. What do you see?
You see a gecko.
It uses its toes to climb trees.
Its brown, bumpy skin makes it
hard to see on a log.

Bengal Tiger

Look closely. What do you see?
You see a Bengal tiger.
Each tiger has a different set of stripes.
The stripes make the tiger
hard to see in tall grass.

Leafy Sea Dragon

Look closely. What do you see?
You see a leafy sea dragon.
Its skin grows flaps that look like
waving seaweed.
Hungry fish do not see
the leafy sea dragon.

Peacock Flounder

Look closely. What do you see?
You see a peacock flounder.
It lives in the sand and mud
under the sea.
Its skin changes color
to look like its home.

Bullfrog

Look closely. What do you see?
You see a bullfrog.
Its dark stripes and yellow-green color
look like water and grass.
It hides well in a pond or stream.

Snow Leopard

Look closely. What do you see?
You see a snow leopard.
It lives in high places with lots of snow.
Its pale fur and dark spots make it
hard to see among snow and rocks.

Chameleon

Look closely. What do you see?
You see a chameleon.
It can be brown on the ground.
It can turn green in a tree.
A chameleon can change
its color quickly!

Snowshoe Hare

Look closely. What do you see?
You see a snowshoe hare.
Its fur is brown in the summer
and white in the winter.
The hare's fur helps it hide
from other animals.

Dik-Dik

Look closely. What do you see?
You see a dik-dik.
It is small and quick.
Its brown fur makes it
hard to see in the woods.

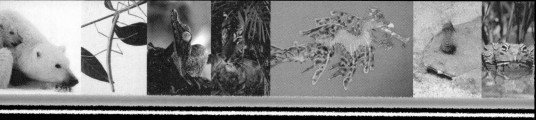

Moth

Look closely. What do you see?
You see a moth.
Its wings are hard to see
next to the gray tree bark.
Its wing spots look like eyes.
The spots scare away birds.

Green Snake

Look closely. What do you see?
You see a green snake.
It is covered with small, hard plates
called *scales*.
Green scales are hard to see
in green leaves.

Snail

Look closely. What do you see?
You see a snail.
It lives in wet, dark places.
It looks for plants to eat at night.
Its small shell is hard to see
in a garden.

LOOK CLOSELY! Hidden Animals
Comprehension Questions

1. Which animal do you think would be the hardest to spot? Which would be the easiest?

2. These animals use camouflage to protect themselves. Do you think camouflage is a good form of protection?

3. Why does white fur make the polar bear hard to see?

4. What feature of the leafy sea dragon makes it hard to spot?

5. Why do you think the peacock flounder was given its name?

6. What happens to the peacock flounder's skin to help it hide?

7. How does a moth scare away birds?

8. What are scales? Which animal has scales?

INTENSE!
Machines

By Teresa Domnauer

Extreme machines do important jobs.
They help people build and explore.
They help people move and travel.
They help people farm and rescue.
They help people have fun, too.

Front-End Loader

This machine is a front-end loader.
You might see one at a building site.
It scoops up huge loads of dirt
with its bucket.
It pours the dirt into a dump truck.

200

Giant Dump Truck

This machine is a giant dump truck.
You might see one at a mine.
It carries huge loads of soil and rocks
in its bed.
It dumps the load wherever
it is needed.

Combine

This machine is a combine.
You might see one at a farm.
It can pick a whole field
of corn in a day.
It takes the kernels off the corn
and collects them in a bin.

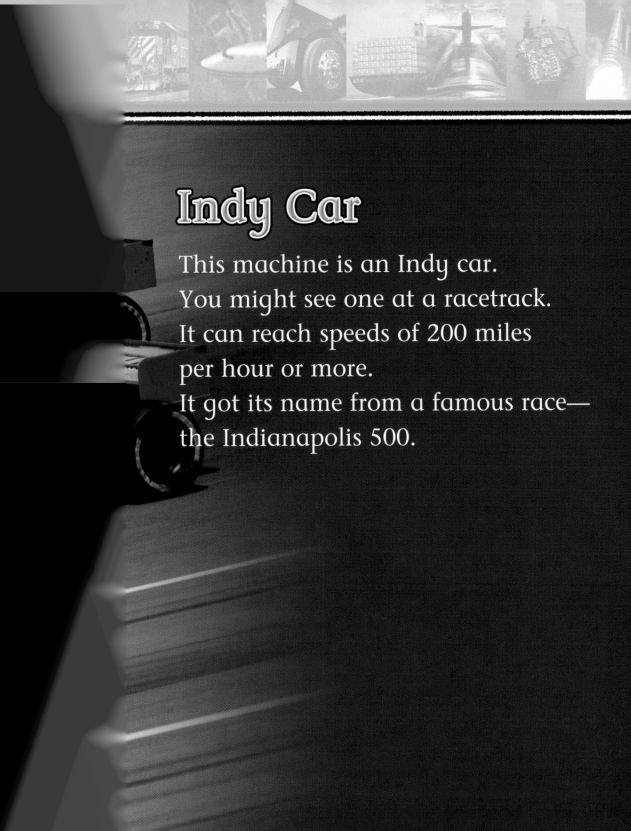

Indy Car

This machine is an Indy car.
You might see one at a racetrack.
It can reach speeds of 200 miles
per hour or more.
It got its name from a famous race—
the Indianapolis 500.

Chopper

This machine is a chopper.
You might see one on the road.
A chopper is a specially built
motorcycle.
It is lighter and faster than most
motorcycles!

Fire Truck

This machine is a fire truck.
You might see one racing
down the street.
It has a ladder that is almost
100 feet long.
The ladder helps firefighters get
to the tops of tall buildings.

Helicopter

This machine is a helicopter.
You might see one flying
over your city.
This kind carries people to the
hospital during an emergency.
Nurses and paramedics ride in it.
They care for the hurt person
during the flight.

Locomotive

This machine is a locomotive.
You might see one zooming
along railroad tracks.
It has a very powerful engine.
It pulls long trains loaded with freight.
It pulls passenger trains, too.

Boeing 747

This machine is a Boeing 747.
You might see one soaring in the sky.
It is a huge jumbo jet
with four engines.
It carries passengers all over the world.
It can even carry a space shuttle
on its back!

Semitruck

This machine is a semitruck.
You might see one on the highway.
It hauls big loads across the country.
Some semitrucks have a bed
behind the driver's seat.
Then, truck drivers can stop and
rest inside.

Cargo Ship

This machine is a cargo ship.
You might see one on the ocean.
It delivers huge amounts of things
all around the world. It carries food,
oil, and many other goods.

Submarine

This machine is a submarine.
You might see one coming up
out of the water.
Its special shape helps it move
smoothly through the water.
Some submarines are used in war.
Others help scientists explore ocean life.

Aircraft Carrier

This machine is an aircraft carrier.
You might see one at a Navy base.
This giant ship carries military planes.
It is so big that planes can take off
and land on its deck.

AMAZING!
Structures

By Katharine Kenah

Table of Contents

There are many amazing creations
on earth.
Some of these creations are man–made.
Thousands of people visit these places
every year.
Have you seen any of these
amazing creations?

Stonehenge

Look at what is in England!
Stonehenge is a very old creation.
It is made of huge stones.
The stones form circles.
Some people think that Stonehenge
was a kind of church.

Pyramid and Great Sphinx

Look at what is in Egypt!
People built this pyramid
over 4,000 years ago.
It is made of thousands of stone blocks.
The blocks are as big and heavy
as trucks.
The Great Sphinx is also very old.
It has the face of a man and the body
of a lion.

Great Wall of China

Look at what is in China!
The Great Wall of China
is the longest creation on earth.
It is about 4,000 miles long.
The wall is so long that it can be seen
from outer space!

Empire State Building

Look at what is in New York!
The Empire State Building is one
of the tallest buildings in the world.
It has 103 floors.
There are 1,860 steps from the bottom
to the top of the building.

Mount Rushmore

Look at what is in South Dakota!
Mount Rushmore is a sculpture
of four American presidents.
Their faces are cut into the side
of a cliff.
It took over ten years to carve
the faces out of the rock!

Golden Gate Bridge

Look at what is in California!
The Golden Gate Bridge is one
of the largest bridges in the world.
It crosses part of the San Francisco Bay.
The Golden Gate Bridge is not gold.
It is really orange!

The White House

Look at what is in Washington, D.C.!
The White House is the home
of the President of the United States.
It has 132 rooms and 35 bathrooms.
The President works on the first floor.
The President's family lives
on the second floor.

Hoover Dam

Look at what is between Nevada
and Arizona!
The Hoover Dam is a huge, high wall.
It is as tall as a 70-story building.
The Hoover Dam crosses
the Colorado River.
Water flows through the dam
and runs machines that make electricity.

Leaning Tower of Pisa

Look at what is in Italy!
The Tower of Pisa is a bell tower.
It is nearly 1,000 years old.
After the Tower of Pisa was built,
it started to tip over.
That was because the ground under it
was soft.
Scientists found ways to keep it
from falling.

Eiffel Tower

Look at what is in Paris, France!
The Eiffel Tower was built
for the World's Fair in 1889.
It is 986 feet tall.
This is about as tall as 170 people!
The tower is made of iron and steel.

Notre Dame

Look at what else is in Paris, France!
Notre Dame is a large, famous church.
It has three big rose windows.
The windows are made of colored glass
and shaped like roses.
Stone animals, called *gargoyles,*
line the edges of the roof.

Windsor Castle

Look at what is close to London!
Windsor Castle is home
to the kings and queens of England.
The castle covers as much ground
as nine football fields.
When the queen is at home,
a special flag flies above the castle.

Neuschwanstein Castle

Look at what is in Germany!
Neuschwanstein Castle was built
for King Ludwig of Bavaria
over 150 years ago.
The castle had running water, toilets,
heat, and bathtubs.
This castle was the model for the
Sleeping Beauty Castle at Disneyland®!

AMAZING! Structures
Comprehension Questions

1. What is Stonehenge made from?

2. How old is the pyramid in Egypt? Do you think it was easy or hard to build?

3. How long is the Great Wall of China?

4. How many steps does the Empire State Building have?

5. Describe Mount Rushmore. Can you name one president who is a part of the sculpture?

6. Where is the Golden Gate Bridge? Why do you think the bridge is famous?

7. Who lives in the White House? Why do you think it is called the White House?

8. What river does the Hoover Dam cross?